Y0-EGD-682

PRE TEEN PRESSURES

STRESS

by Barbara Sprung

RSVP

RAINTREE
Steck-Vaughn
PUBLISHERS
The Steck-Vaughn Company

Austin, Texas

Consultants
Pamela Holmer, Social Worker, Family Service Association of Bucks County, PA
William B. Presnell, Clinical Member, American Association for Marriage and Family Therapy

Developed for Steck-Vaughn Company by
Visual Education Corporation, Princeton, New Jersey
Project Director: Jewel Moulthrop
Editor: Paula McGuire
Editorial Assistant: Jacqueline Morais
Photo Research: Sara Matthews
Electronic Preparation: Cynthia C. Feldner, Manager; Elaine Weiss
Production Supervisor: Ellen Foos
Electronic Production: Lisa Evans-Skopas, Manager; Elise Dodeles, Deirdre Sheean, Isabelle Verret
Interior Design: Maxson Crandall

Raintree Steck-Vaughn Publishers staff
Editor: Kathy DeVico
Project Manager: Joyce Spicer

Photo Credits: Cover: © Robert W. Ginn/Unicorn Stock Photos; 6: © Tony Freeman/PhotoEdit; 10: © Richard Hutchings/PhotoEdit; 13: © David Young-Wolff/PhotoEdit; 16: © The Kobal Collection; 23: © Michelle Bridwell/PhotoEdit; 27: © Mary Kate Denny/PhotoEdit; 29: © Tony Freeman/PhotoEdit; 33: © Jeff Greenberg/Unicorn Stock Photos; 35: © Mary Kate Denny/PhotoEdit; 37: © Michelle Bridwell/PhotoEdit; 43: © Tony Freeman/PhotoEdit

Library of Congress Cataloging-in-Publication Data
Sprung, Barbara.
    Stress/by Barbara Sprung.
       p.   cm. — (Preteen pressures)
    Includes bibliographical references and index.
    Summary: Discusses some of the different things that cause stress for preteens, and suggests ways to cope.
    ISBN 0-8172-5033-6
    1. Stress in children—Juvenile literature. 2. Stress management for children—Juvenile literature. [1. Stress (Psychology)] I. Title. II. Series.
BF723.S75S68 1998
155.4′18—dc21
                                       97-29471
                                          CIP
                                          AC

Printed and bound in the United States
1 2 3 4 5 6 7 8 9 0 LB 01 00 99 98 97

CONTENTS

INTRODUCTION

People seem to use the word *stress* often these days. You hear adults talk about feeling stress at work or from their family responsibilities. Preteens talk about being "stressed out" over their homework or pressures from their friends. When people feel stress, they are responding to sudden physical or mental demands. Their bodies may react in certain ways. They may feel afraid or uncomfortable, tired or even sick. Or they may find surprising physical or mental strengths and abilities that they didn't know they had. Not all stress is harmful.

Reading this book will help you understand stress. You will learn what causes stress and how it affects the way we feel and act. Today all of us—adults, teens, and preteens—are living in a time of stressful events. Preteens in other times did not have an easy life either. Some young people had to travel long distances to school, often on foot. Some even had to leave school altogether to work on farms and in factories so that their families could survive. Like kids today, they probably felt pressure to do well in school, felt competitive with other students, and sometimes suffered from teasing and bullying. They, too, were confused by the physical changes in their bodies. And sometimes they had to deal with difficult situations at home, such as abuse or alcoholism.

So there is nothing new about stress. It has always been part of life. But life today is very different from that of long ago. Kids today face problems that may have been unknown to young people in the past, such as:

▶ Violence in their neighborhoods, on TV, and in movies (even imaginary violence can make us feel stress about our safety)

▶ Too much emphasis on sex at an early age

▶ Pressure from other kids to use drugs or join a gang

▶ Family problems caused by drug addiction, abuse, or divorce

This book will pay particular attention to these problems and provide you with some useful tips on dealing with the many kinds of stress that you may experience. You can't avoid stress—it is part of life. But you can learn to recognize it, and you can take steps to control it.

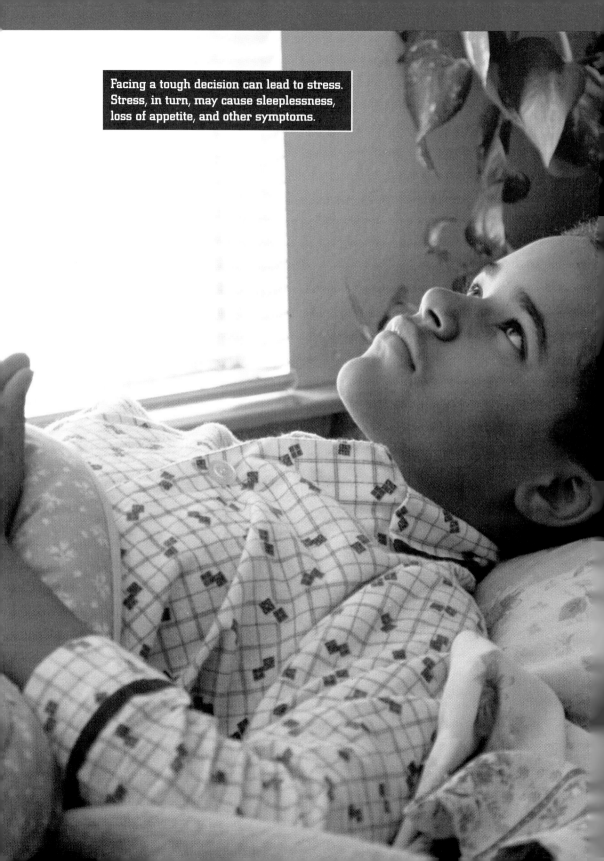

Facing a tough decision can lead to stress. Stress, in turn, may cause sleeplessness, loss of appetite, and other symptoms.

WHAT IS STRESS?

Tim, who is 12, has been lying on his bed and staring at the ceiling for hours. His friends are planning to do something really dumb. And he is worried.

Tim's friends are going to light firecrackers and put them in people's mailboxes. Tim knows this is dangerous and destructive, because some kids once did it to his mailbox, and his parents were furious. His parents reported it to the police.

Tim knows that the guys will be angry if he doesn't join them. They'll probably tease him a lot and call him a wimp in front of everyone at school. Tim doesn't know what to do. He didn't sleep very well last night. He wasn't even hungry at lunchtime. Every time he thinks about his problem, his stomach aches.

Tim's dilemma is causing him to feel stress. If he decides to go along with his friends, he may be in serious trouble. If he decides not to go along, he may lose some of his friends. Whichever decision he makes, the consequences will be negative.

Stress is our bodies' reaction to sudden physical or mental demands or to changes in our routines. These demands or changes are called stressors. And the emotions that we feel as a result of these stressors are part of the stress. Moving to a new city, going out on a first date, experiencing the death of a parent, living close to a noisy highway day in and day out—any of these situations may cause stress.

THE SIGNS OF STRESS

Usually when we describe stress, we talk about how it makes us feel. In other words, we describe the symptoms of stress. Some of those feelings or symptoms are a pounding heart; cold, clammy hands; sweaty palms; a dry mouth and a choking feeling; a queasy stomach or cramps. Stress can make you feel some or all of these.

Other people might notice some signs of stress that you may not be aware of yourself. A doctor testing your blood pressure would probably find that it is higher than usual. Your face might redden from a sudden flow of blood toward your head. Or the blood might seem to drain from your face so that you grow pale.

STRESS AND THE BODY'S REACTION

Stress disrupts the normal internal balance of the body. As soon as the body senses a change, whether it is sudden or has been happening over a long time, our internal systems respond. Certain glands (such as the pituitary and adrenal glands) produce increased amounts of powerful hormones. Hormones are chemical substances in the body that affect the activities of cells and organs. Hormones control important processes, such as growth, development, reproduction, and our response to stress. Of course, most of us don't go around thinking about how our glands and hormones are working. But we certainly do feel their effects on our bodies.

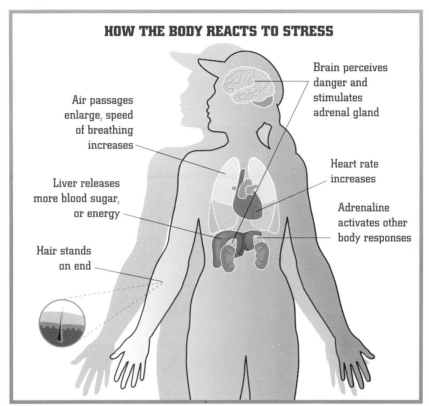

HOW THE BODY REACTS TO STRESS

Brain perceives danger and stimulates adrenal gland

Air passages enlarge, speed of breathing increases

Heart rate increases

Liver releases more blood sugar, or energy

Adrenaline activates other body responses

Hair stands on end

NEGATIVE STRESS

If we are suddenly frightened, for example, our muscles tighten. We may not be able to move quickly or even breathe easily. When that happens we feel tense—a very common symptom of stress. We say that we "feel stress" or that we "are stressed" when we are in scary or unhappy situations. This negative type of stress is called distress.

In some situations the feeling of tension can become so great that the body reacts by becoming physically ill. This happens when the body's immune system (the body's defense against disease) just can't keep up with the level of stress. But that is not usually the case. In most situations our glands produce whatever extra amounts of hormones are needed to keep us from reacting in an extreme way.

POSITIVE STRESS

Although stress can make us feel pretty uncomfortable at times, it does have a positive side. Sometimes when we have a challenge to meet, like winning a race or an

essay contest, stress causes us to work harder. Hormones give us the extra energy to achieve our goals. Sometimes stress helps us stand up to people who want us to do the wrong thing. And sometimes stress helps us think of ways to solve problems so that the stressful feelings will disappear. Stress that

Not all stress is bad. Stress can give people the extra boost they need to meet certain challenges.

motivates us to do our very best is positive. Stress that comes from an exciting, pleasurable, or positive feeling is called eustress.

But most of us don't think about stress when we are in happy situations. We just feel good or excited, and we enjoy those feelings.

STRESS FOR PRETEENS

Stress is a part of every person's life from infancy through old age. The preteen years are a time when you are going through rapid physical and emotional growth. And this may cause you to feel stressed. Maybe your parents have been pushing you to get good grades since kindergarten, and you feel pressure to succeed. It was easy in elementary school, but now is a different story. The work is tough, and, frankly, you feel like dropping out. You're not sure what you're able to do or even what you want to do.

Perhaps you've just moved to town from another part of the country. Things are very different at your new school. The kids dress in a more relaxed way, act more boldly, and seem more grown-up than the kids did in your old school. You feel shy about talking to them. You'd really like to make new friends, but you're embarrassed and can hardly work up the nerve to approach anyone.

Hold on! There are some ways you can learn to deal with stress like this. As we discuss various stressful situations in the pages ahead, we'll also point out ways to stay healthier and happier in the midst of them.

CHANGING BODIES AND PUBERTY

"I'm Josh. I'm very good at basketball. But I'm worried because I'm real short, and I don't see myself growing very much. I don't look like I'm nearly 12, even though I'm one of the oldest kids in the fifth grade. It's OK now, because my friends like me. Suppose when I go to middle school next year they call me 'Shrimp' or 'Shorty' or something? That would really be embarrassing, and I'm already stressing out about it.

My dad told me he didn't start really growing until he was over 14, and he's pretty tall now. I hope the same thing happens to me. One of my grandfathers really is a shrimp, and the other one is not very tall either.

I've been noticing something in my class. The girls seem much older than the boys. Some are much bigger than even the tallest boys. I hope things even out in middle school."

PUBERTY

Josh is feeling some of the normal stress of puberty. Puberty begins around age 11 (sometimes earlier, sometimes later). During puberty the sexual organs

Preteens who experience puberty later than their peers often worry that they will be teased.

of boys and girls begin to grow to maturity, and their bodies change in many other ways, too. But puberty is about much more than body changes. It's about emotions, feelings, mood changes, and sexual urges. It's also about sometimes feeling confused and uncomfortable. In short, puberty can be a time of stress.

Sometimes during puberty, you may feel as if you can't control the way you act. Maybe you sometimes scream at your parents, sister, or brother. Then you are sorry the minute the words are out of your mouth. If that happens, you can apologize later. But recognizing that you are feeling stress is the first step toward dealing with it.

Learning about puberty is really important. Ask your parents or an adult you trust to talk to you about it. Your school librarian can recommend good books on the subject. Understanding what is happening to you and your friends, both girls and boys, will help you deal better with the stress you sometimes feel. Talking to your friends about what is going on in your lives will also help. Remember, they are going through some of the same things.

SEXUALITY

Laurie, Pamela, Keesie, and Maureen are sitting in a booth at the pizza restaurant near their school. A bunch of middle school kids hang out there after school. Usually the girls sit at one table and the boys at another. But they call out stuff to each other. Sometimes it's fun, and sometimes it's embarrassing.

Today Mike, an eighth grade guy, yelled out to Keesie, "Hey, chick, wanna do it with me?" Keesie did not know what to do. Her face turned red, and she couldn't think of anything to say back to him. The other girls just laughed, which didn't help.

Larry and Jason were sitting with Mike. Larry said, "I'd like to do it with Keesie, too. She turns me on."

"You wouldn't even know how," said Jason.

"That's what you think," Larry snapped. "I've done it lots of times."

Jason and Mike said at the same time, "Oh, yeah? Done what?"

"Had sex with girls," Larry answered. But he kept his head down and looked a little embarrassed.

"You mean you wish you did," said Mike with a sneer.

Thinking and talking about sex becomes important in the preteen years, especially with the onset of puberty. It is natural at this time for preteens to take an interest in sex. Your bodies are changing, and you want to talk about what is happening to you.

When girls or boys hang out and talk about sex, they sometimes exaggerate how much they have actually experienced. It becomes a kind of bragging game. One boy might say, "I made it with Amy." Another might retort, "So what? I've done it with lots of girls." A girl might tell her friends that she went "all the way" with some very popular boy.

For both boys and girls, trying to seem cool about sex can be a great source of stress. It's not easy to deal with the changes that are occurring in your body.

MIXED MESSAGES

In our society today, messages about sex are everywhere. They are in advertisements, in magazines, and on TV. They are in the words of songs, in music videos, and even in toys. We are encouraged to dress a certain way, walk a certain way, talk a certain way—all aimed at making us "sexy."

At the same time, though, we receive other messages, and they are equally strong. Sex is not something you talk about. When we learn about the human body in school, our sexual parts (called genitals) are often left out of the lessons. The baby dolls that little children play with look a lot like real babies, except that they don't have genitals.

Although there is often sexual content in movies, on television, and in advertisements, sex may not be discussed by parents or other adult authority figures. The mixed messages that result can cause confusion, especially for preteens.

Many adults seem embarrassed when children show curiosity about sex or about the sexual parts of their bodies. And many parents are uncomfortable talking to their children about sex. These parents may provide very little information. They may make sex seem secret, private, and something that is not discussed openly. They probably didn't talk about sex in their own families when they were young.

So how come we can hear all this sexy stuff on TV, in ads, and in song lyrics, but we can't talk openly about sex? How will young people learn how to be responsible about their sexuality? Read on!

HAVING CONFLICTS

The mixed messages we receive about sex can be very confusing. And the confusion can lead to conflict and stress. Many preteens know deep down that developing a loving relationship is as important as having sex. However, the conflict between their deepest beliefs and the need to be like everybody else can be overwhelming. The struggle to resist the unexpected physical urges of their bodies and the pressure of friends may cause a great deal of stress. Feelings of fear and anxiety and even such symptoms as lack of hunger or nausea can take over and cause severe emotional and physical distress.

SEXUAL PEER PRESSURE

Giving in to peer pressure means that you will do anything your friends do or urge you to do. If you let it, peer pressure can push you into having sex before you are ready.

Sometimes friends will dare you, beg you, or try to scare you into doing what they are doing. They'll try to make you feel like an outsider if you don't follow their lead. Some kids will even pressure their friends to do what they haven't done themselves. (Remember that some kids exaggerate or brag.)

Peer pressure about sex can be very tough to resist. Stress can be extreme. Try getting together with some friends who share your feelings. Discuss ways to stop or resist this kind of pressure. Find out if your school has a program that teaches how to cope with peer pressure.

SEXUAL RESPONSIBILITY

An interest in sex is perfectly natural during puberty. Learn about yourself and your emotions. Take the time to understand who you are and how you feel about sex. Ask for information, or read books about the sexual experience. Learn about the consequences of sexual behavior and how to protect yourself from both pregnancy and disease.

If you are tempted to have sex for the first time, it is a good idea to talk it over first with your partner. Make sure you and your partner are in agreement about it. Are you certain that he or she thinks it is a good idea? Do you both know what it means to have safer sex? Have you thought about how you will act and where it will take place? Maybe you aren't as comfortable about it as you thought you were. If not, don't worry about admitting your doubts; you won't be the first. Better to speak up sooner rather than later, when it may be too late.

By resolving in advance your own possible conflicts about sex, by resisting unwanted peer pressure, you may avoid worse stress in the future. Human sexuality is a broad and complicated topic. The more you know about it, the better you will understand its complications. Let's talk about three special sexual issues: homosexuality, sexual abuse, and sexual harassment. These are situations with which you may need immediate help.

BEING HETEROSEXUAL OR HOMOSEXUAL

Part of understanding human sexuality is learning about heterosexuality and homosexuality. Heterosexuality means that the partners in a sexual relationship are male and female. Homosexuality means that the partners are of the same sex, either two males or two females. Two female partners are also called lesbians.

Being heterosexual or being homosexual is part of who you are, not something you learn. Both heterosexuals and homosexuals have been around since the world began. But in our society, there is a lot of prejudice against homosexuals. They are often teased and bullied. Many are the victims of hatred and violence. Sometimes even parents have a hard time accepting that their child is homosexual.

Being homosexual often means living with a great deal of stress. This is true of homosexuals at any age—preteen, teen, and adult. At the time when young people are becoming sexually mature, they may be confused about their sexual orientation. Those who believe that they are homosexual may be afraid to express their feelings openly. They learn very quickly that if they do, they will be the target of jokes, insults, or worse. This fear causes severe stress that may go on for a long time.

SEXUAL ABUSE AND SEXUAL HARASSMENT

In recent years there have been many stories in the newspapers and on TV about sexual abuse and sexual harassment. Sexual abuse and sexual harassment are related, but they are not the same. Sexual abuse means that someone forces a person to have sex against that person's will. Touching or fondling a person against his or her will is also considered sexual abuse. If someone forces you to perform a sexual act, that is sexual abuse. If someone teases you about sex or makes sexual remarks that you find disturbing, that is sexual harassment. Sexual harassment is less serious, but it is still not acceptable.

Sexual abuse and sexual harassment have been around for a long time. But in the past, those subjects were kept secret. No one talked about such things. If you were a victim of abuse or harassment, you were expected to suffer in silence. But now sexual abuse and sexual harassment are against the law.

Sometimes people (especially children) who are sexually abused actually feel guilty about it. They think that somehow the abuse is their own fault. Or they are afraid to talk about it because their abuser has threatened them in some way. Abusers want you to feel guilty and afraid. They think that then you won't tell anyone.

Sexual abuse and sexual harassment are the negative side of human sexuality. To be a victim of either of them can cause great stress at any age. But we have made some progress. It is no longer a secret topic, and help is available.

WHAT TO DO

Being homosexual, being sexually abused, and being sexually harassed are stressful situations that require help from people you trust. Here are some things you can do immediately:

▶ If you know that you are homosexual, or think that you might be, ask an adult you trust for advice. This person can guide you to an organization that can help you understand your sexual orientation. There are many groups that provide information and guidance for homosexual youth. You can find information about these groups in the telephone book, in the library, and at the back of this book.

▶ If you are sexually abused by anyone (even a family member or someone else you know well), seek help right away from an adult who you know will take you seriously. Don't be afraid to tell on someone who has abused you, because what that person is doing is wrong and is against the law. You are not to blame.

▶ If you feel that you are being sexually harassed, take the same steps as for sexual abuse. Sexual harassment is serious. Like sexual abuse, it is against the law and must be stopped right away.

MORE ABOUT PEER PRESSURE

Melissa and Sharon are best friends. They walk home from school together every day past the town park. Some kids from the middle school hang out in the park after school and on weekends. Every day someone in the crowd invites Melissa and Sharon to join in. Some of the most popular kids in the fifth and sixth grades are part of this crowd. They know all the latest dances. They wear cool clothes. And they smoke cigarettes and drink beer.

Melissa and Sharon really want to join the crowd. They know that it would be fun to be part of the most popular group of kids. They want to dance and be cool. What they don't want to do is smoke or drink beer.

Melissa and Sharon are very confused, and the confusion is causing them stress. They want to be "in," but they know that the kids in the crowd won't think they are cool if they refuse to smoke and drink. They don't know what to do.

It's OK to want to be part of a crowd, but choose a crowd that respects your values and won't pressure you to do things you don't want to do.

Melissa and Sharon are dealing with peer pressure, the feeling that they must do what the others are doing, even though it goes against what they know is right. Peer pressure is one of the most stressful parts of being a preteen or a teenager. Sometimes kids dare you to do things you know are wrong. Your friends may tease you and call you names because you resist their dares. They don't make it easy for you to say no. If they were honest with themselves, they probably would admit that what they are daring you to do is harmful. They are most likely going against personal or family beliefs or school rules. If you say no, you might make them feel uncomfortable or stressed about what they are doing.

WHEN TO FOLLOW THE CROWD

Is it always a bad idea to follow the crowd? Of course not. It feels good to have friends and to have a sense of belonging. If your family doesn't notice that you are growing up and have your own ideas, your friends certainly do. They are going through the same thing with their families. Dressing like your friends or having the same hairstyle creates a sense of belonging. Listening to the same music gives everyone something to talk about together. And hanging out together is just a lot of fun. It feels good, and it feels right.

Going along with the crowd is not a question of never or always. It is a question of balance. Sometimes you have to dare to be different. If your friends start doing things that can lead you into trouble, don't join in. Try telling them straight out that you won't go along, and why. They may respect you more. Or you may lose some of them as friends. That can be really tough to take. Like Melissa and Sharon, you have to make a decision. Do you really want friends who don't respect your values? Do you really want friends who do dumb or dangerous things?

WHAT TO DO ABOUT IT

There are several ways to have a sense of belonging without falling into the trap of peer pressure. Here are a few suggestions to start you thinking about what will work best for you:

- Develop a strong interest in something (music, astronomy, dramatics, computers, sports, writing, science, or anything else you like). Find friends with similar interests.
- Find one or two close friends instead of a whole crowd.
- Join clubs at school or in your church, synagogue, or mosque.

Signs of Stress

Your body may react with:
- a pounding heart
- shortness of breath
- dry mouth
- sweating
- a headache
- an upset stomach and vomiting
- diarrhea or constipation
- tense muscles
- a skin rash
- trembling
- a rise in heart rate or blood pressure

Your emotions may be:
- nervousness
- anger and impatience
- lack of concentration
- worry
- forgetfulness
- loss of interest

Your behavior may include:
- crying
- sleep problems
- restlessness
- loss of appetite or overeating
- hurrying or talking too fast
- criticizing others
- avoiding family and friends

Reactions to prolonged stress:
- severe fatigue
- colds or other illnesses
- asthma
- injuries from accidents due to loss of attention
- depression
- suicide attempts

▶ Go to an after-school program at your neighborhood community center. Adult counselors can help you identify your interests and pursue them.

The best way to overcome peer pressure as a pre-teen is to think for yourself. Learn what peer pressure is and how it is affecting your life. Then you can decide when it's OK to go along with the crowd and when it is wrong or dangerous. Watch for signs of stress as you think about the decision you are about to make. Sometimes it takes courage to say no, but you can do it.

BULLIES AND BULLYING

A bully is a person who picks on someone else whom he or she thinks of as weaker. Usually a bully looks for someone who is smaller or younger, or who seems different in some way from most other kids. A bully can hurt you physically by hitting, pushing, or tripping you. He or she can hurt your feelings by insulting you. A bully can scare you with threats. Bullies like to feel that they have power over other people. It makes them feel important.

Bullying often occurs during the preteen years and causes a lot of stress for kids that age. However, bullies can be any age. Some children begin to bully others as early as preschool. If their bullying behavior is not stopped, they become the bullies we all know in third grade, sixth grade, or any grade. Adults have to teach kids that being a bully is very harmful to others and not a good way to make yourself feel powerful. And by the way, adults who never learned that lesson themselves can be bullies also.

Being bullied can cause a lot of stress at any age.

HOW BEING BULLIED MAKES YOU FEEL

Bullies pick on others because it makes them feel powerful and in control. Being bullied makes you feel just the opposite way—powerless and out of control. It's called being a victim. Just about all the feelings that go with being a victim are stressful. Your stomach may hurt. Your heart may pound. You may have a headache. You might feel nervous, scared, or angry. You might also feel helpless, especially if you can't think of a way to stop the bully. Stopping a bully (or bullies) is not easy, but there are actions you can take.

WHAT TO DO ABOUT BULLYING

Adults often tell kids that they have to stand up to a bully. Yell and fight back. Comics, movies, and TV programs show these ways to stop being a victim. In stories, bullies usually back down when someone finally stands up to them. But in real life, it doesn't always work that way. Usually a kid who is being bullied needs some help to stop the bully.

Researchers have been studying bullying. They have come up with ideas that you might find helpful. Some of these ideas have come from the preteens they interviewed:

▶ Schools should have a No Bullying Allowed rule that is strictly enforced by the principal and all the other adults in the school. If bullying is not tolerated, it stops. If your school doesn't have this rule, you might want to gather a group of kids to talk to your teacher or the principal about writing one together.

▶ If your school has no such rule and won't write one, here are some actions you can take if you are being bullied:

1. Talk to the bully in person. Let him or her know that the bullying is hurting you, and that you want it to stop. (Hitting back or using other forms of violence often leads to more violence.) Use strong words and a strong voice.

2. Write a letter to the bully, telling him or her how you feel. Again, use strong words. Let the bully know that you are angry and that you expect the bullying to stop.

3. Your school may have a conflict resolution or peer mediation program. Such programs provide special training to students to help them solve problems that arise among their peers. If your

school has a program, use it to help you solve your problem with the bully or bullies.

4. Seek help from an adult. If someone tells you to "work it out yourself," find another adult who <u>will</u> take some action.

5. This step is for a person who is a bully. You probably know that it's wrong to pick on or hurt kids who are younger or smaller than you. Even though you may feel powerful for a little while if someone is afraid of you, way down deep it probably doesn't really feel so good. Just like the victims of bullying, you need to find an adult to help you learn how to feel powerful and in control without bullying. Think about it. Try it.

Some schools use peer mediation to handle the problems of teasing and bullying.

TEASING AND TEASERS

"Hi, I'm Carrie, and I'm in fifth grade. I feel so bad today, I can't even do my work. My teacher has already told me twice that I should stop staring out the window and finish my assignment. The reason I feel so bad is that these two girls in my class, Jessica and Tanya, have been teasing me again. It started on the school bus this morning. When I got on the bus, they yelled out, 'Here comes two-ton; watch the bus sink.' That started all the kids laughing. I wished I could become invisible.

I know I'm overweight, and I'm trying to diet. But being teased all the time about my weight really hurts me inside. Sometimes it makes me forget that I can play the piano, and that I'm very good in math. Why can't Jessica and Tanya find out about the real me? One thing's for sure. I'm never ever going to tease another kid. I know how it feels."

Teasing is a lot like bullying, but without the physical violence. Usually a teaser makes a person feel bad by using words, picking on something about her or him that seems different. In Carrie's case, she weighed more than the other girls in her class. Other kids might be teased for having big feet, or large ears, or because they are new immigrants to the United States, or because they are different in some other way from most of the kids in the school. Boys tease other boys, girls tease other girls, and boys and girls tease each other. But no matter who is doing the teasing, it hurts another person. Teasing may not hurt you physically the way bullying sometimes does, but it can hurt your feelings very deeply. Sometimes kids are teased so much that they are afraid to go to school.

Teasing is another cause of stress. You will probably feel embarrassed or angry, maybe blush or get tears in your eyes. If it continues, you may even feel sick to your stomach and want to stay home from school.

WHY DO PEOPLE TEASE?

Some people tease because it makes them feel powerful to put down someone else. They are pretty much like bullies. Most people, however, think that teasing is a kind of joking and that everyone does it. Adults often tell kids that teasing is a normal part of growing up, so they shouldn't let it bother them. You have probably been told something like, "You should learn to take it," or "Be a good sport."

Lots of times it is adults who tease kids. Usually they don't mean to be hurtful, but do it in a joking way. Maybe it's a dad who calls his daughter "Skinny" or his son "Goofy" as a kind of pet name. Maybe it's a big sister who says, "Come on, Stupid, I'll take you to the mall."

HOW TEASING MAKES YOU FEEL

Even though we may try to ignore this kind of teasing, it never makes us feel good about ourselves. Sometimes it makes us feel really bad to be called "Skinny," "Goofy," or "Stupid," but we don't say anything or try to stop the teasing. We also may think that, since we have been teased and have learned to be a good sport, it's OK to tease others.

But is it really OK? Remember how awful Carrie feels when she is teased about her weight? It almost makes her forget about all the things she does well. It lowers her self-esteem (her good feelings about herself). Teasing causes stress; and stress makes you feel rotten. Feeling that way for a long time is harmful.

DON'T BE A BYSTANDER

A bystander is a person who watches an event but doesn't do anything about it. Being a bystander can be stressful—especially when you see something happening that you know is wrong. It can make you feel ashamed or weak. If you see someone your own age or younger being teased, you don't have to stand by and do nothing. You can tell the teaser to stop. If possible, ask some friends to back you up. The teaser may respond better if a few kids give the same "stop" message. If that doesn't work, seek help from an adult.

If you make up your mind that teasing is bad for everyone—the person being teased, the teaser, and the bystanders—you have the power to stop it.

Teasing is hurtful. It makes a person angry and lowers his or her self-esteem.

TO STOP TEASING

To stop someone from teasing you, follow the steps for stopping a bully. Let the person know how the teasing makes you feel. If that doesn't work, seek help from an adult who understands your feelings.

If you are doing the teasing, think about how you would feel if someone was teasing you. Examine your reasons for teasing. Are you taking out your own stress on someone else? If so, there are healthier ways to deal with your stress. There are some tips on page 39.

FAMILY PROBLEMS

The minute Danny walked in the door after school, he felt his stomach go into a knot. The apartment was a total mess. Ashtrays full of smelly cigarette butts sat on every table. The kitchen sink was piled high with dirty dishes. Danny's father was asleep in the family room. Danny knew that his dad had been drinking again.

Danny had a ton of homework. But he knew he would have to clean up the kitchen and make some dinner for himself before he could start to do it. If this day was like the others, his dad would wake up about seven o'clock. He would make up some story about why he had fallen asleep. But Danny would be able to smell the liquor on his breath.

Danny had been dealing with this problem for over a year, ever since his mother left and his dad lost his job. Danny felt sorry for his dad. He missed his mom. He felt angry because his dad wasn't taking charge. And he felt very stressed. How could he keep up his schoolwork when he was worried and angry all the time? He was lonely, too. How could he ever bring a friend home to this mess?

Danny knew that he needed some help, but he didn't have a clue about where to go to find it. He couldn't wait until he was old enough to leave home.

A parent's alcoholism can create a wide range of problems for a child, such as being ashamed to bring friends home.

DRUG ABUSE

Families have always had problems. Some of the problems may have been different in other times. But whatever they were, they usually had a bad effect on the children.

Some of the problems families faced in the past are the same ones that families face today. Alcoholism has been a problem throughout history, and in just about every country in the world. When adults drink too much, they often lose control and sometimes abuse their children or spouses (wives or husbands). They may also neglect their responsibilities—family, home, and job. This situation puts an unfair burden on their children, as in Danny's case.

Today we know that alcohol and many other drugs are addictive, or habit-forming. This means that once a person begins to use the drug, his or her body becomes dependent on it. The need for the drug becomes so strong that an addicted person will do almost anything to satisfy that need.

We know that people who are addicted commit crimes to get the money to buy more alcohol or other drugs, such as marijuana, cocaine, and heroin. We know that drug dealers bring about violence. They make our neighborhoods unsafe to live in. That's why buying, selling, or using these drugs is illegal. Illegal drugs have become one of the major problems of our time. Drug abuse destroys individuals, families, and neighborhoods.

DIVORCE

Another family problem that many of today's kids have to deal with is divorce. Although many people in earlier times were unhappily married, they seldom divorced. Divorce was generally considered unacceptable or shameful. Also, laws were different, so that a divorce was difficult to obtain.

The inability to divorce was hard on families. Kids certainly knew when their parents did not get along or love each other. However, the typical American family stayed together. Both parents were around. Today one parent may live in a different house or apartment or even in a different town or state from the rest of the family. Some parents seldom see their children.

Katie stood by as her mother spoke to her dad on the phone.

"Look, George, it's your weekend, and you promised you'd be there for Katie. I have plans for the weekend, and it's simply not convenient for me to have her around. Besides, she has been looking forward to seeing you, though I can't imagine why. What do you mean, you have a plane to catch? Hey, that's not fair! Wait, George! . . . Darn it, he hung up.

"Well, Katie. Your father's done it again! Think you can plan a sleepover at someone's house on Saturday?"

When parents share custody, kids are sometimes caught in the middle.

Can you imagine how Katie felt? Sometimes kids are caught in the middle of their parents' arguments. If divorced parents share custody (care and control), their kids may live in two places. They may shift from one parent's house to the other's every week or even every few days. Many kids see one parent only on weekends. It can be very stressful to have to "visit" your own parent. And it's even worse if the arrangements break down.

Katie dreads the conversations between her parents. Her feelings of fear, loneliness, and rejection are very stressful, and she is desperate for some kind of relief and help.

VIOLENCE

Domestic violence (physically hurting one's spouse or children) is another serious problem of our time. Domestic violence usually occurs as a result of stress caused by other problems. Alcoholism, drug addiction, or an unhappy marriage can lead to violent outbursts. Other causes might be stress from working long hours or from being hassled on the job, lack of money for the family's needs, or an inability to control angry feelings.

Domestic violence is frightening to witness. It can cause serious injuries and a huge amount of stress. Kids are often helpless to protect themselves or a parent who is being beaten. And they are embarrassed or afraid to ask for help. As with the stress of other family problems, however, help is available. There are steps you can take to relieve the stress of even the worst situations.

Tips on Managing Stress

▶ Exercise daily, and eat plenty of vegetables and fruit. Eating nutritious foods and staying healthy will reduce the effects of strain on your body.

▶ Organize your time. Think ahead, and try not to take on more than you can accomplish. Realistic goals will reduce anxiety and stress.

▶ Just hang out sometimes. Listen to music, or play games on the computer. Give yourself a little break when you're feeling tense or upset.

▶ Learn your own limits. Sometimes you have to say no, even to activities you enjoy. Being overtired invites stress.

▶ Remember that sometimes things do go wrong, in spite of your best efforts. Learn how to accept and cope with occasional disappointments.

▶ Try to change the way you think about yourself. Boost your self-image, and learn to laugh at things. Don't be your own worst enemy.

▶ Learn ways to relax. Here are a few: Try lying on the floor and relaxing each part of the body, one by one, working from your feet up to your neck. This can be helpful in bed when you are trying to go to sleep. Take deep breaths. Stretch your face muscles in as many ways as you can (this may make you laugh, if you use a mirror), then relax them.

▶ Think about a place you like very much, such as the beach, the mountains, or a secret hideout. Close your eyes for a few minutes, and imagine that you are there.

▶ When things are really rough, you can learn to spot the signs of stress and recognize your reactions. Try to think calmly about the problem that you are facing and what, if anything, you can possibly do about it. Make a decision, and then act on it. Your best decision may be to ask for help.

FAMILY STRESS AFFECTS YOU

Sometimes adults think that kids—including pre-teens—are unaware of family problems. Some families try to hide their problems. They pretend that everything is OK. In truth, even very young children notice and are affected by family problems. They may not be able to express their feelings in words, but they cry a lot, show anger, or become depressed.

Preteens and teenagers certainly know when their families are in trouble. Remember Danny? He had to deal with his father's unhappiness and alcoholism every day. When families are under stress, kids are under stress.

IT'S A BURDEN

Sometimes having family problems to cope with makes you feel as if you are carrying a gigantic load of stones up a very steep hill. In other words, it's a heavy burden. It may seem to you that other kids have it so easy. They may not. They may be hiding problems, too. It's hard to concentrate on schoolwork if you are worried that your mom, dad, brother, or sister is taking drugs. Anger or confusion about your parents' divorce can really make you feel down. If you have been a victim of domestic violence, you may be injured. You may also be embarrassed to go to school with bruises.

If you are facing any of these kinds of family problems, and lots of kids do, you may feel that you have to grow up too fast. You are right. Having to take on adult responsibilities when you are young is very stressful.

WHAT TO DO ABOUT IT

There is another way to look at your situation. Learning about stress, and ways to manage it, can make you feel more confident. Confidence will enable you to cope with your problems or find the help you need. Sometimes you can learn what not to do from the problems in your own family. For example, Danny may not want to drink at all, after seeing how alcohol has affected his father.

Learning to cope with your stress doesn't mean that you will not need help with your family's problems. Sometimes it is really hard to talk to outsiders about family troubles. It's embarrassing. You may feel like a tattletale. You may even feel afraid to tell. But telling someone can be the first step toward solving the problem that is causing you so much stress.

You are the best person to judge whether you need help with a family problem. And because you know that there is a problem, you are the one who will need the courage to ask a trusted adult for help. Be assured that there are people around who can help you. You will find a list of places to go to find help at the end of this book.

A FINAL LOOK AT STRESS

By now one thing should be clear. Stress is a part of everyday life. Even small things—like losing your favorite pen—can be stressful. Stressful events occur at home, at school, and in your community. Stress in one person's life affects family members also. Stress that affects your friends may affect the friendship. Stressful events that occur in the world—a war, an airplane disaster, or a hurricane—may affect you, too. What affects you most, however, are the stressful things that happen to you as an individual.

This book was written to help you understand that there are two sides to stress. The "up" side is that stress can make you work harder and accomplish more than you thought you could.

The "down" side is that dealing with stress can be difficult, even painful. Negative stress often doesn't go away by itself. Here are some suggestions to help you cope with stressful situations you may face in your preteen years.

TALK ABOUT IT

It is rarely a good idea to hide your feelings. People often feel better when they have someone they can talk to about what's bothering them. Practice saying the

Communicating with people about your feelings is one of the best ways of coping with stressful situations.

words that communicate what is on your mind. Communication will help you get through life. It's a skill you will always find useful.

SEEK HELP

It's a good idea to have a special friend, someone you can talk to comfortably. It should be a person you can trust and who will listen, answer questions, and take what you say seriously. This person can be a parent, an older friend, a guidance counselor, a priest, a minister, or a rabbi. There are people and programs to help you in every community. Many people care about what happens to you.

Some preteens find that keeping a journal is helpful. You can write down the thoughts and feelings you have about the problems that cause you to feel stressed. Writing poems, stories, or songs is another way to express your feelings and relieve stress. If you have artistic ability, painting and drawing are also good outlets for stress.

Identifying your interests and following them is a great way to deal with the stresses of the preteen years. Young people are talented in a whole variety of areas: music, dance, drama, sports, chess, carpentry, computers, fishing, rocketry, to name just a few. Developing a strong interest gives you a ready-made group of friends who like the same activities you do. It keeps you busy and involved. Most of all, it makes you feel good about yourself and the things you can accomplish.

Finally, beginning to know who you are and how you react to certain situations may help you avoid unwanted stress. If you know that getting a low grade in school makes you feel bad, you might ask yourself why. Is it important to you to do better, or do you fear your parents' reaction? If you understand why you feel the way you do, you may be able to deal with (or avoid) another low grade.

Discovering what is important for you, where your values lie, and just what is finally obtainable will help you make difficult choices and resolve conflicts. Just remember that stress is a part of your life, but you can learn how to deal with it.

addiction: A physical or mental dependence on a substance, such as alcohol or another drug.

adrenal gland: The gland above the kidneys that secretes adrenalin, the hormone that provides extra energy during emergencies.

blood pressure: The pressure of the blood against the inner walls of arteries; can vary according to age, health, and levels of stress or excitement.

bystander: A person who watches an event but does not participate or do anything about it.

conflict resolution: Identifying a conflict and attempting to solve the problem through reason and communication.

heterosexuality: Having feelings for and being sexually attracted to members of the opposite sex.

homosexuality: Having feelings for and being sexually attracted to members of the same sex.

mixed messages: Conflicting signals or information from different sources, such as parents and the media, about an issue.

peer pressure: The feeling that one should do what others are doing; the urging of friends to behave as they do.

pituitary gland: The gland, located beneath the brain, that controls growth and development; called the master gland because it regulates other glands.

puberty: The stage of life at which a person first becomes capable of producing offspring and starts experiencing physical changes in his or her body; occurs at about age 11 for girls and 14 for boys.

sexual abuse: Touching or using a person in an unwanted sexual way; forcing a person to have sexual intercourse.

sexual harassment: Unwanted sexual attention, such as being teased about sex or having to listen to disturbing sexual remarks.

sexuality: Physical and mental qualities that define one's sexual needs and desires.

stressors: The physical or mental demands that trigger stress.

WHERE TO GO FOR HELP

A quick and easy way to find help is to look in your local telephone directory. Many directories have special sections in the white pages or yellow pages under such topics as Alcohol Abuse, Child Abuse, Drug Abuse, and Suicide. Most of the organizations listed have toll-free 800 numbers.

Abuse

National Council on Child Abuse and Family Violence
1155 Connecticut Avenue, NW
Washington, DC 20036
1-800-222-2000

Addiction/Alcoholism

Al-Anon and Alateen
1600 Corporate Landing Parkway
Virginia Beach, VA 23456
1-800-563-1600

National Institute on Drug Abuse
1-800-662-HELP
(662-4357)

Health

HIV/AIDS Hot line
1-800-440-8336

MedSupport FSF International
3132 Timberview Drive
Dunedin, FL 34698

Teens/TAP
1-800-234-8336

Runaways

Child Find, Inc.
P.O. Box 277
New Paltz, NY 12561
1-800-I-AM-LOST (426-5678)

National Runaway Switchboard
Hot line: 1-800-621-4000

The Nine-Line
1-800-999-9999

Sexuality

The Hetrick Martin Institute, Inc.
Two Astor Place
New York, NY 10003
212-674-2400

Sexuality Information and Education Council of the United States (SIECUS)
130 West 42nd Street, Suite 2500
New York, NY 10036
212-819-9770

Suicide/Depression

Father Flanagan's Boystown Crisis Prevention Hotline:
1-800-448-3000

FOR MORE INFORMATION

Fiction

Anderson, Peggy King. *Safe at Home.* Atheneum, 1992.

Blume, Judy. *Then Again, Maybe I Won't.* Bradbury, 1971.

Carbone, Elisa Lynn. *My Daddy's Definitely Not a Drunk.* Waterfront Books, 1992.

Jordan, Mary Kay. *Losing Uncle Tim.* Illustrated by Judith Friedman. Albert Whitman and Co., 1989.

Mead, Alice. *Walking the Edge.* Albert Whitman and Co., 1995.

Vigna, Judith. *My Big Sister Takes Drugs.* Albert Whitman and Co., 1990.

Nonfiction

Gilbert, Sara. *Get Help: Solving the Problems in Your Life.* Morrow Junior Books, 1989.

Harris, Robie H. *It's Perfectly Normal.* Illustrated by Michael Emberly. Candlewick, 1994.

Lee, Richard S., and Mary Price Lee. *Nicotine and Caffeine.* Rosen, 1994.

O'Neill, Catherine. *Focus on Alcohol.* Illustrated by David Neuhaus. Twenty-First Century, 1990.

Rosenberg, Maxine B. *Not My Family: Sharing the Truth about Alcoholism.* Bradbury, 1988.

Seixas, Judith S. *Living with a Parent Who Drinks Too Much.* Greenwillow, 1979.

———. *Living with a Parent Who Takes Drugs.* Greenwillow, 1989.

Terkel, Susan N., and Janice E. Rench. *Feeling Safe and Strong: How to Avoid Sexual Abuse and What to Do If It Happens to You.* Lerner, 1984.

INDEX

abuse, 4, 5, 35, 38, 40. *See also* sexual abuse
addiction, 5, 36, 38
alcoholism, 4, 35, 36, 38, 40
anger, 27, 28, 31, 34, 37, 40
appetite, loss of, 6, 7, 17

belonging, sense of, 11, 17, 22, 24–25

causes (of stress). *See* stressors
communication, 13–14, 16, 17, 18, 20–21, 28–29, 32–33, 41, 42–43
conflict, inner, 7, 16–17, 18, 22, 23, 37–38
conflict resolution, 28–29, 44

decision making, 6, 7, 17–18, 22–25, 26, 39
distress, 9–10. *See also* stressors; symptoms
divorce, 5, 36–38
drinking, 22, 34, 41. *See also* alcoholism
drugs, 5, 36, 38, 40

fear, 4, 9, 17, 20, 27, 38, 41
friends, 4, 7, 11, 14, 17, 22–25, 32, 34, 35, 44. *See also* peer pressure

glands, 8–9
guilt, 20

help, asking for, 20–21, 29, 33, 41, 43
heterosexuality, 18
homosexuality, 18–19, 20–21
hormones, 8–9

information, seeking, 13–14, 17–18, 20–21, 41

living arrangements, 36–38

mediation, 28–29
mixed messages, 15–16
moving, 8, 11

peer pressure, 4, 7, 17, 18, 22–25, 26
physical changes. *See* puberty; symptoms
power-tripping, 26–27, 29, 31
problem solving, 10, 28–29, 32–33
puberty, 12–14, 15–18

responsibility, 4, 16, 17–18, 32, 34, 35

self-esteem, 32, 33, 39, 41, 44
sexual abuse, 18, 19–20, 21
sexual harassment, 19, 20, 21
sexuality, 12–21
shame, 32, 35, 36
sickness, 4, 10, 17, 31
sleeplessness, 6, 7
smoking, 22, 34
standing up for oneself, 10, 24, 26, 27–28, 32–33, 39
stress, negative. *See* stressors; symptoms
stress, positive, 10–11, 41, 42
stressors, 4–5, 7–8, 11, 42
    bullying, 26–27, 29
    family problems, 34–35, 36–38, 40
    sexual issues, 12–14, 15–18, 19–20
    teasing, 30–31, 33
support groups, 21, 43, 46
symptoms (of stress), 4, 6–7, 8, 9–11, 13, 17, 27, 30–32, 34, 38, 40

teasing, 4, 7, 12, 13, 14, 19, 20, 23, 29, 30–33
tension, 9, 10, 39

unhappiness, 9, 32, 36, 38, 40

values, 17, 24, 44
victim, being a, 19–20, 26–27, 30–32, 38, 40
violence, 5, 19, 26, 28, 36, 38, 40

worry, 7, 12, 18, 34, 40